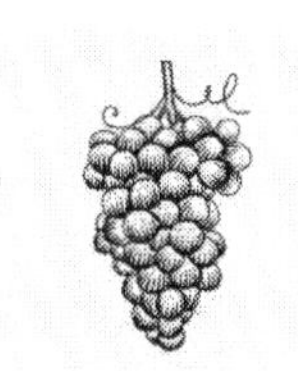

WINE TASTING Journal

Index of Wine Log

N°	Wine name

Nº	Wine name

Nº	Wine name

Nº	Wine name

N° ____

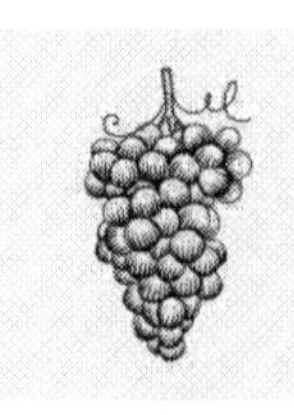

Wine name: ______________________

Red / Rosé / White (circle one) Vintage: ____________

Varietal: ____________________ Alcohol %: ____________

Region/Country: ____________ Winery: ____________

	1	2	3	4	5
Apparence					
Aroma					
Body					
Taste					
Finish					

Aging (years)

0-5 ○ 5-10 ○ 10-15 ○ +15 ○

Review

Tasting Experience ☆ ☆ ☆ ☆ ☆

Quality-Price Ratio ☆ ☆ ☆ ☆ ☆

Buy it again ? ____________________

Notes

____

____

____

N° ____

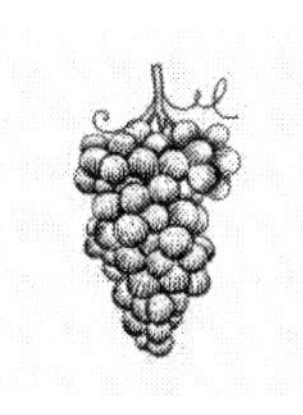

Wine name: ______________________________

Red / Rosé / White (circle one) Vintage: ____________
Varietal: ____________________ Alcohol %: ____________
Region/Country: ____________ Winery: ____________

	1	2	3	4	5
Apparence					
Aroma					
Body					
Taste					
Finish					

Aging (years)

0-5 ○ 5-10 ○ 10-15 ○ +15 ○

Review

Tasting Experience ☆ ☆ ☆ ☆ ☆

Quality-Price Ratio ☆ ☆ ☆ ☆ ☆

Buy it again ? ____________________

Notes

____

____

____

N° ______

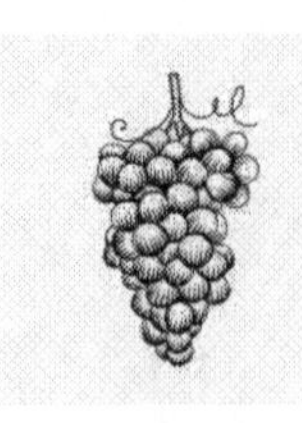

Wine name: ______________________

Red / Rosé / White (circle one) Vintage: ____________

Varietal: ____________________ Alcohol %: ____________

Region/Country: ____________ Winery: ____________

	1	2	3	4	5
Apparence					
Aroma					
Body					
Taste					
Finish					

Aging (years)

0-5 ○ 5-10 ○ 10-15 ○ +15 ○

Review

Tasting Experience ☆ ☆ ☆ ☆ ☆

Quality-Price Ratio ☆ ☆ ☆ ☆ ☆

Buy it again ? ____________________

Notes

____

____

____

N° ____

Wine name: ______________________

Red / Rosé / White (circle one) Vintage: __________
Varietal: ______________ Alcohol %: __________
Region/Country: __________ Winery: __________

	1	2	3	4	5
Apparence					
Aroma					
Body					
Taste					
Finish					

Aging (years)

0-5 ○ 5-10 ○ 10-15 ○ +15 ○

Review

Tasting Experience ☆ ☆ ☆ ☆ ☆

Quality-Price Ratio ☆ ☆ ☆ ☆ ☆

Buy it again ? ______________

Notes

____

____

____

N° ______

Wine name: ____________________

Red / Rosé / White (circle one) Vintage: ____________

Varietal: ____________________ Alcohol %: ____________

Region/Country: ____________ Winery: ____________

	1	2	3	4	5
Apparence					
Aroma					
Body					
Taste					
Finish					

Aging (years)

0-5 ○ 5-10 ○ 10-15 ○ +15 ○

Review

Tasting Experience ☆ ☆ ☆ ☆ ☆

Quality-Price Ratio ☆ ☆ ☆ ☆ ☆

Buy it again ? ____________________

Notes

____

____

____

N° ______

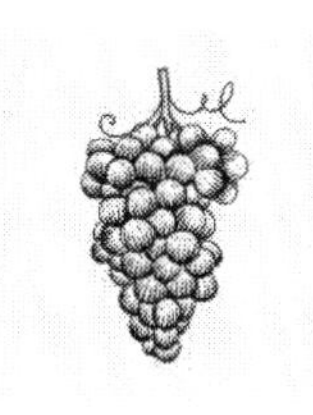

Wine name: ______________________

Red / Rosé / White (circle one) Vintage: ______

Varietal: ______________ Alcohol %: ______

Region/Country: __________ Winery: ______

	1	2	3	4	5
Apparence					
Aroma					
Body					
Taste					
Finish					

Aging (years)

0-5 ○ 5-10 ○ 10-15 ○ +15 ○

Review

Tasting Experience ☆ ☆ ☆ ☆ ☆

Quality-Price Ratio ☆ ☆ ☆ ☆ ☆

Buy it again ? ______________

Notes

____

____

____

N° ____

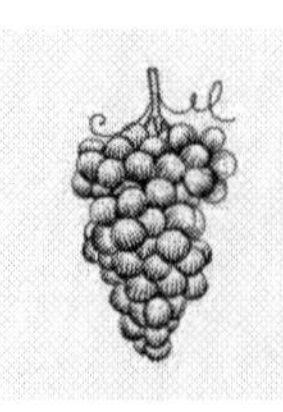

Wine name: ______________________

Red / Rosé / White (circle one) Vintage: ____________

Varietal: ______________________ Alcohol %: ____________

Region/Country: ______________ Winery: ____________

	1	2	3	4	5
Apparence					
Aroma					
Body					
Taste					
Finish					

Aging (years)

0-5 ○ 5-10 ○ 10-15 ○ +15 ○

Review

Tasting Experience ☆ ☆ ☆ ☆ ☆

Quality-Price Ratio ☆ ☆ ☆ ☆ ☆

Buy it again ? ______________________

Notes

____

____

____

N° ______

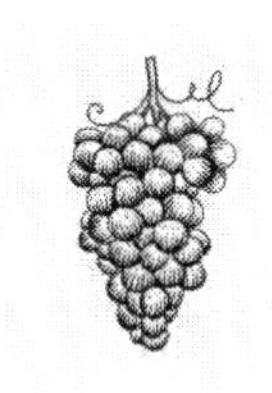

Wine name: ______________________

Red / Rosé / White (circle one) Vintage: ______

Varietal: ______________ Alcohol %: ______

Region/Country: ______________ Winery: ______

	1	2	3	4	5
Apparence					
Aroma					
Body					
Taste					
Finish					

Aging (years)

0-5 ○ 5-10 ○ 10-15 ○ +15 ○

Review

Tasting Experience ☆ ☆ ☆ ☆ ☆

Quality-Price Ratio ☆ ☆ ☆ ☆ ☆

Buy it again ? ______________

Notes

____

____

____

N° ____

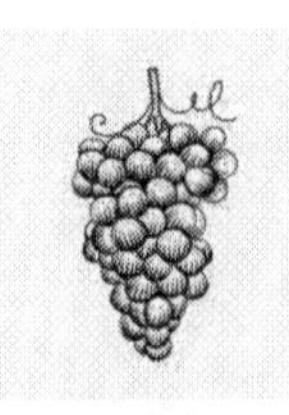

Wine name: ______________________

Red / Rosé / White (circle one) Vintage: __________
Varietal: ____________________ Alcohol %: __________
Region/Country: ______________ Winery: __________

	1	2	3	4	5
Apparence					
Aroma					
Body					
Taste					
Finish					

Aging (years)

0-5 ○ 5-10 ○ 10-15 ○ +15 ○

Review

Tasting Experience ☆ ☆ ☆ ☆ ☆

Quality-Price Ratio ☆ ☆ ☆ ☆ ☆

Buy it again ? ____________________

Notes

____

____

____

N° ____

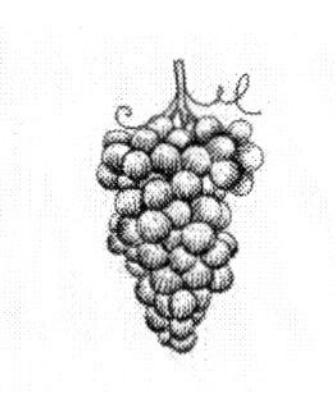

Wine name: ____________________

Red / Rosé / White (circle one) Vintage: ____________
Varietal: ____________ Alcohol %: ____________
Region/Country: ____________ Winery: ____________

	1	2	3	4	5
Apparence					
Aroma					
Body					
Taste					
Finish					

Aging (years)

0-5 ○ 5-10 ○ 10-15 ○ +15 ○

Review

Tasting Experience ☆ ☆ ☆ ☆ ☆

Quality-Price Ratio ☆ ☆ ☆ ☆ ☆

Buy it again ? ____________

Notes

____

____

____

N° ____

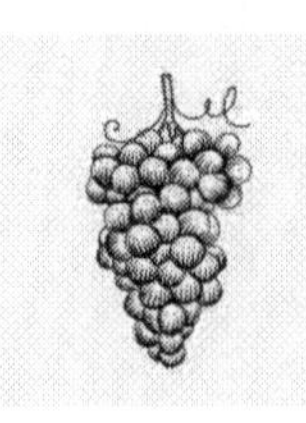

Wine name: ________________

Red / Rosé / White (circle one) Vintage: ________

Varietal: ________________ Alcohol %: ________

Region/Country: ____________ Winery: ________

	1	2	3	4	5
Apparence					
Aroma					
Body					
Taste					
Finish					

Aging (years)

0-5 ○ 5-10 ○ 10-15 ○ +15 ○

Review

Tasting Experience ☆ ☆ ☆ ☆ ☆

Quality-Price Ratio ☆ ☆ ☆ ☆ ☆

Buy it again ? ________________

Notes

____

____

____

N° ____

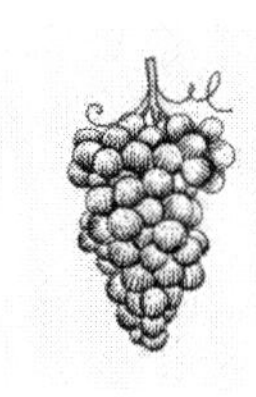

Wine name: ____________________

Red / Rosé / White (circle one) Vintage: ____________

Varietal: ____________ Alcohol %: ____________

Region/Country: ____________ Winery: ____________

	1	2	3	4	5
Apparence					
Aroma					
Body					
Taste					
Finish					

Aging (years)

0-5 ○ 5-10 ○ 10-15 ○ +15 ○

Review

Tasting Experience ☆ ☆ ☆ ☆ ☆

Quality-Price Ratio ☆ ☆ ☆ ☆ ☆

Buy it again ? ____________

Notes

____

____

____

N° ____

Wine name: ____________________

Red / Rosé / White (circle one) Vintage: __________
Varietal: __________ Alcohol %: __________
Region/Country: __________ Winery: __________

	1	2	3	4	5
Apparence					
Aroma					
Body					
Taste					
Finish					

Aging (years)

0-5 ○ 5-10 ○ 10-15 ○ +15 ○

Review

Tasting Experience ☆ ☆ ☆ ☆ ☆

Quality-Price Ratio ☆ ☆ ☆ ☆ ☆

Buy it again ? __________

Notes

____

____

____

N° ______

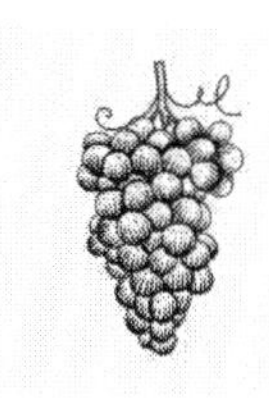

Wine name: ______________________________

Red / Rosé / White (circle one) Vintage: __________

Varietal: __________________ Alcohol %: __________

Region/Country: ____________ Winery: __________

	1	2	3	4	5
Apparence					
Aroma					
Body					
Taste					
Finish					

Aging (years)

0-5 ○ 5-10 ○ 10-15 ○ +15 ○

Review

Tasting Experience ☆ ☆ ☆ ☆ ☆

Quality-Price Ratio ☆ ☆ ☆ ☆ ☆

Buy it again ? ____________________

Notes

____

____

____

N° ______

Wine name: ______

Red / Rosé / White (circle one) Vintage: ______
Varietal: ______ Alcohol %: ______
Region/Country: ______ Winery: ______

	1	2	3	4	5
Apparence					
Aroma					
Body					
Taste					
Finish					

Aging (years)

0-5 ○ 5-10 ○ 10-15 ○ +15 ○

Review

Tasting Experience ☆ ☆ ☆ ☆ ☆

Quality-Price Ratio ☆ ☆ ☆ ☆ ☆

Buy it again ? ______

Notes

______

______

______

N° ______

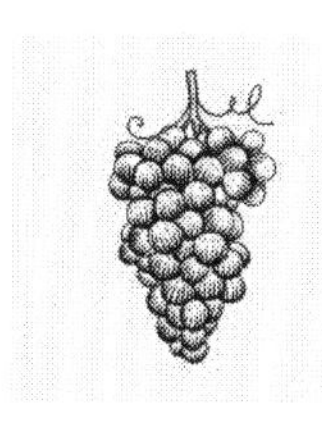

Wine name: ______________________

Red / Rosé / White (circle one) Vintage: ______
Varietal: ______________ Alcohol %: ______
Region/Country: ______________ Winery: ______

	1	2	3	4	5
Apparence					
Aroma					
Body					
Taste					
Finish					

Aging (years)

0-5 ○ 5-10 ○ 10-15 ○ +15 ○

Review

Tasting Experience ☆ ☆ ☆ ☆ ☆

Quality-Price Ratio ☆ ☆ ☆ ☆ ☆

Buy it again ? ______________

Notes

____

____

____

N° ____

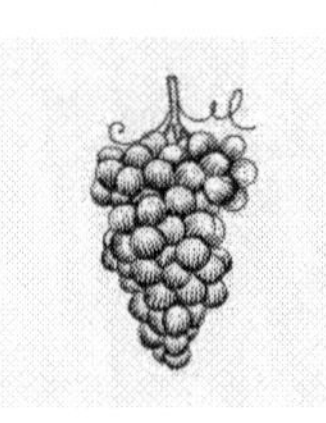

Wine name: ____________________

Red / Rosé / White (circle one) Vintage: ____________
Varietal: ____________________ Alcohol %: ____________
Region/Country: ____________ Winery: ____________

	1	2	3	4	5
Apparence					
Aroma					
Body					
Taste					
Finish					

Aging (years)

0-5 ○ 5-10 ○ 10-15 ○ +15 ○

Review

Tasting Experience ☆ ☆ ☆ ☆ ☆

Quality-Price Ratio ☆ ☆ ☆ ☆ ☆

Buy it again ? ____________________

Notes

____

____

____

N° ____

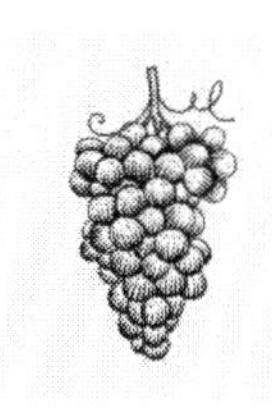

Wine name: ____________________

Red / Rosé / White (circle one) Vintage: ________
Varietal: ______________ Alcohol %: ________
Region/Country: ______________ Winery: ________

	1	2	3	4	5
Apparence					
Aroma					
Body					
Taste					
Finish					

Aging (years)

0-5 ◯ 5-10 ◯ 10-15 ◯ +15 ◯

Review

Tasting Experience ☆ ☆ ☆ ☆ ☆

Quality-Price Ratio ☆ ☆ ☆ ☆ ☆

Buy it again ? ______________

Notes

____

____

____

N° ____

Wine name: ____________________

Red / Rosé / White (circle one) Vintage: ________
Varietal: ________________ Alcohol %: ________
Region/Country: ________ Winery: ________

	1	2	3	4	5
Apparence					
Aroma					
Body					
Taste					
Finish					

Aging (years)

0-5 ○ 5-10 ○ 10-15 ○ +15 ○

Review

Tasting Experience ☆ ☆ ☆ ☆ ☆

Quality-Price Ratio ☆ ☆ ☆ ☆ ☆

Buy it again ? ________________

Notes

____

____

____

N° ______

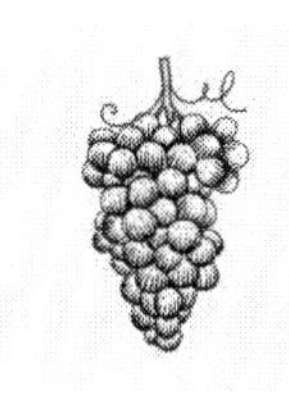

Wine name: ______________________

Red / Rosé / White (circle one) Vintage: __________

Varietal: ______________ Alcohol %: __________

Region/Country: __________ Winery: __________

	1	2	3	4	5
Apparence					
Aroma					
Body					
Taste					
Finish					

Aging (years)

0-5 ○ 5-10 ○ 10-15 ○ +15 ○

Review

Tasting Experience ☆ ☆ ☆ ☆ ☆

Quality-Price Ratio ☆ ☆ ☆ ☆ ☆

Buy it again ? ______________

Notes

____

____

____

N° ____

Wine name: ____________________

Red / Rosé / White (circle one) Vintage: ____________
Varietal: ____________ Alcohol %: ____________
Region/Country: ____________ Winery: ____________

	1	2	3	4	5
Apparence					
Aroma					
Body					
Taste					
Finish					

Aging (years)

0-5 ○ 5-10 ○ 10-15 ○ +15 ○

Review

Tasting Experience ☆ ☆ ☆ ☆ ☆

Quality-Price Ratio ☆ ☆ ☆ ☆ ☆

Buy it again ? ____________

Notes

____

____

____

N° ____

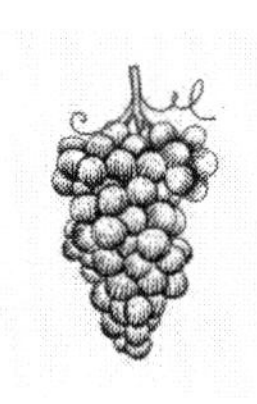

Wine name: ______________________

Red / Rosé / White (circle one) Vintage: __________

Varietal: ______________ Alcohol %: __________

Region/Country: ______________ Winery: __________

	1	2	3	4	5
Apparence					
Aroma					
Body					
Taste					
Finish					

Aging (years)

0-5 ○ 5-10 ○ 10-15 ○ +15 ○

Review

Tasting Experience ☆ ☆ ☆ ☆ ☆

Quality-Price Ratio ☆ ☆ ☆ ☆ ☆

Buy it again ? ______________

Notes

____

____

____

N° ____

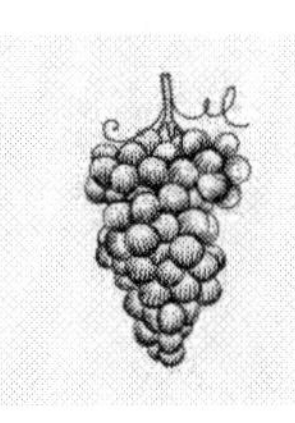

Wine name: ____________________

Red / Rosé / White (circle one) Vintage: ____________
Varietal: ____________ Alcohol %: ____________
Region/Country: ____________ Winery: ____________

	1	2	3	4	5
Apparence					
Aroma					
Body					
Taste					
Finish					

Aging (years)

0-5 ○ 5-10 ○ 10-15 ○ +15 ○

Review

Tasting Experience ☆ ☆ ☆ ☆ ☆

Quality-Price Ratio ☆ ☆ ☆ ☆ ☆

Buy it again ? ____________

Notes

____

____

____

N° ____

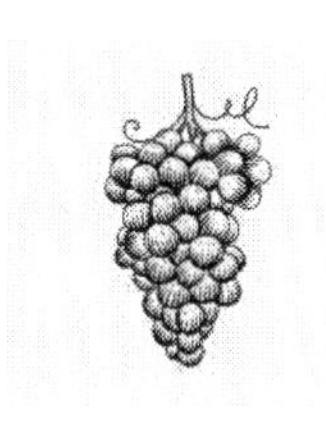

Wine name: ____________________

Red / Rosé / White (circle one) Vintage: ____________

Varietal: ____________ Alcohol %: ____________

Region/Country: ____________ Winery: ____________

	1	2	3	4	5
Apparence					
Aroma					
Body					
Taste					
Finish					

Aging (years)

0-5 ○ 5-10 ○ 10-15 ○ +15 ○

Review

Tasting Experience ☆ ☆ ☆ ☆ ☆

Quality-Price Ratio ☆ ☆ ☆ ☆ ☆

Buy it again ? ____________

Notes

____

____

____

N° ____

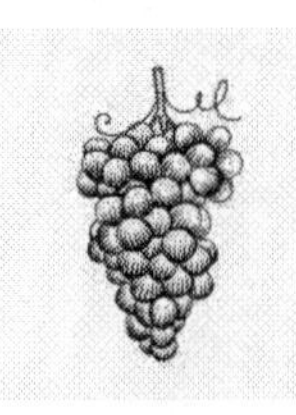

Wine name: ____________________

Red / Rosé / White (circle one) Vintage: ________
Varietal: ____________ Alcohol %: ________
Region/Country: ____________ Winery: ________

	1	2	3	4	5
Apparence					
Aroma					
Body					
Taste					
Finish					

Aging (years)

0-5 ○ 5-10 ○ 10-15 ○ +15 ○

Review

Tasting Experience ☆ ☆ ☆ ☆ ☆

Quality-Price Ratio ☆ ☆ ☆ ☆ ☆

Buy it again ? ____________

Notes

____

____

____

N° ____

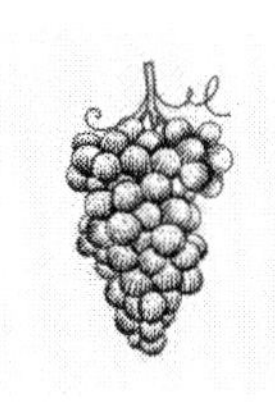

Wine name: ______________________

Red / Rosé / White (circle one) Vintage: ____________

Varietal: ____________ Alcohol %: ____________

Region/Country: ____________ Winery: ____________

	1	2	3	4	5
Apparence					
Aroma					
Body					
Taste					
Finish					

Aging (years)

0-5 ○ 5-10 ○ 10-15 ○ +15 ○

Review

Tasting Experience ☆ ☆ ☆ ☆ ☆

Quality-Price Ratio ☆ ☆ ☆ ☆ ☆

Buy it again ? ____________

Notes

____

____

____

N° ____

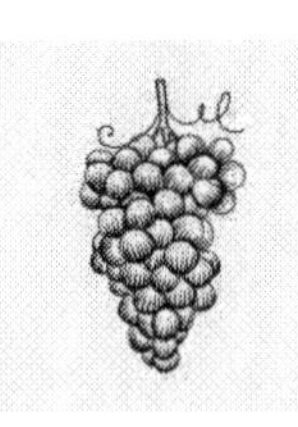

Wine name: ______________________

Red / Rosé / White (circle one) Vintage: __________
Varietal: ______________ Alcohol %: __________
Region/Country: __________ Winery: __________

	1	2	3	4	5
Apparence					
Aroma					
Body					
Taste					
Finish					

Aging (years)

0-5 ○ 5-10 ○ 10-15 ○ +15 ○

Review

Tasting Experience ☆ ☆ ☆ ☆ ☆

Quality-Price Ratio ☆ ☆ ☆ ☆ ☆

Buy it again ? ______________

Notes

____

____

____

N° ______

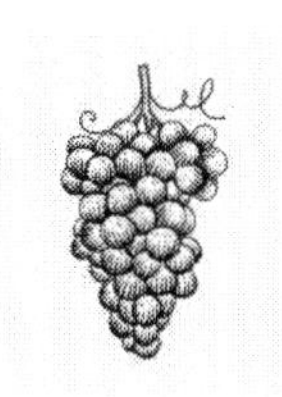

Wine name: ______

Red / Rosé / White (circle one) Vintage: ______

Varietal: ______ Alcohol %: ______

Region/Country: ______ Winery: ______

	1	2	3	4	5
Apparence					
Aroma					
Body					
Taste					
Finish					

Aging (years)

0-5 ○ 5-10 ○ 10-15 ○ +15 ○

Review

Tasting Experience ☆ ☆ ☆ ☆ ☆

Quality-Price Ratio ☆ ☆ ☆ ☆ ☆

Buy it again ? ______

Notes

______

______

______

N° ____

Wine name: ______________________

Red / Rosé / White (circle one) Vintage: __________
Varietal: ______________ Alcohol %: __________
Region/Country: __________ Winery: __________

	1	2	3	4	5
Apparence					
Aroma					
Body					
Taste					
Finish					

Aging (years)

0-5 ○ 5-10 ○ 10-15 ○ +15 ○

Review

Tasting Experience ☆ ☆ ☆ ☆ ☆

Quality-Price Ratio ☆ ☆ ☆ ☆ ☆

Buy it again ? ______________

Notes

____

____

____

N° ____

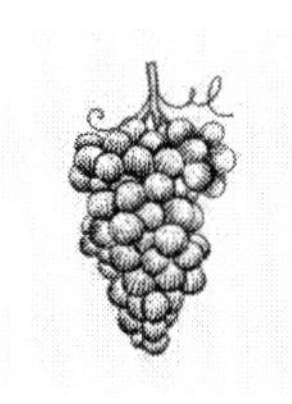

Wine name: ______________________

Red / Rosé / White (circle one) Vintage: __________

Varietal: ______________ Alcohol %: __________

Region/Country: __________ Winery: __________

	1	2	3	4	5
Apparence					
Aroma					
Body					
Taste					
Finish					

Aging (years)

0-5 ○ 5-10 ○ 10-15 ○ +15 ○

Review

Tasting Experience ☆ ☆ ☆ ☆ ☆

Quality-Price Ratio ☆ ☆ ☆ ☆ ☆

Buy it again ? ______________

Notes

____

____

____

N° ____

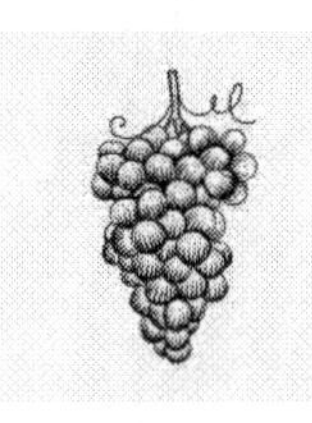

Wine name: ______________________

Red / Rosé / White (circle one) Vintage: ____________

Varietal: ____________ Alcohol %: ____________

Region/Country: ____________ Winery: ____________

	1	2	3	4	5
Apparence					
Aroma					
Body					
Taste					
Finish					

Aging (years)

0-5 ○ 5-10 ○ 10-15 ○ +15 ○

Review

Tasting Experience ☆ ☆ ☆ ☆ ☆

Quality-Price Ratio ☆ ☆ ☆ ☆ ☆

Buy it again ? ____________

Notes

____

____

____

N° ______

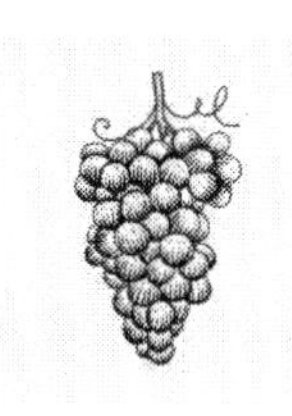

Wine name: ______________________________

Red / Rosé / White (circle one) Vintage: __________

Varietal: ______________________ Alcohol %: __________

Region/Country: ______________ Winery: __________

	1	2	3	4	5
Apparence					
Aroma					
Body					
Taste					
Finish					

Aging (years)

0-5 ○ 5-10 ○ 10-15 ○ +15 ○

Review

Tasting Experience ☆ ☆ ☆ ☆ ☆

Quality-Price Ratio ☆ ☆ ☆ ☆ ☆

Buy it again ? ______________________

Notes

____

____

____

N° ____

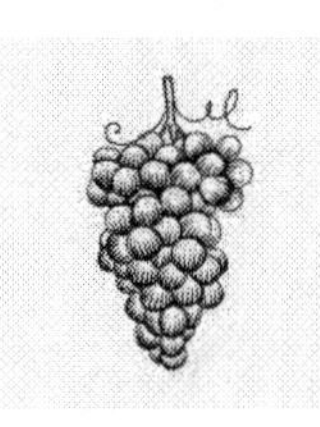

Wine name: ______________________

Red / Rosé / White (circle one) Vintage: ____________

Varietal: ______________ Alcohol %: ____________

Region/Country: ______________ Winery: ____________

	1	2	3	4	5
Apparence					
Aroma					
Body					
Taste					
Finish					

Aging (years)

0-5 ○ 5-10 ○ 10-15 ○ +15 ○

Review

Tasting Experience ☆ ☆ ☆ ☆ ☆

Quality-Price Ratio ☆ ☆ ☆ ☆ ☆

Buy it again ? ______________

Notes

____

____

____

N° ____

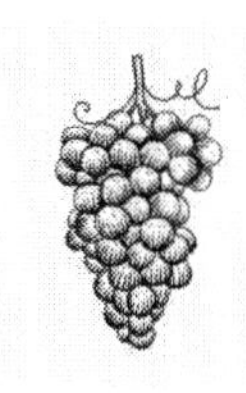

Wine name: ____________________

Red / Rosé / White (circle one) Vintage: ________
Varietal: ________________ Alcohol %: ________
Region/Country: ____________ Winery: ________

	1	2	3	4	5
Apparence					
Aroma					
Body					
Taste					
Finish					

Aging (years)

0-5 ○ 5-10 ○ 10-15 ○ +15 ○

Review

Tasting Experience ☆ ☆ ☆ ☆ ☆

Quality-Price Ratio ☆ ☆ ☆ ☆ ☆

Buy it again ? ________________

Notes

____

____

____

N° ____

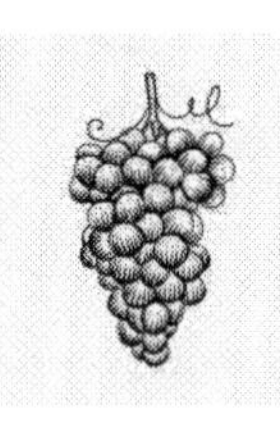

Wine name: ______________________

Red / Rosé / White (circle one) Vintage: __________
Varietal: ______________ Alcohol %: __________
Region/Country: ______________ Winery: __________

	1	2	3	4	5
Apparence					
Aroma					
Body					
Taste					
Finish					

Aging (years)

0-5 ◯ 5-10 ◯ 10-15 ◯ +15 ◯

Review

Tasting Experience ☆ ☆ ☆ ☆ ☆

Quality-Price Ratio ☆ ☆ ☆ ☆ ☆

Buy it again ? ______________

Notes

____

____

____

N° ______

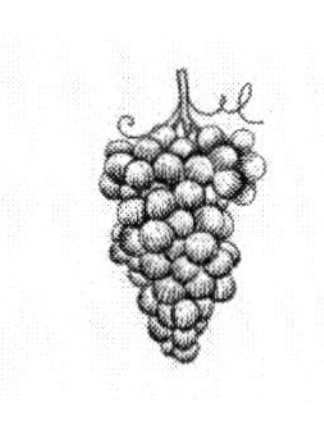

Wine name: ______________________

Red / Rosé / White (circle one) Vintage: ______

Varietal: ______________ Alcohol %: ______

Region/Country: ______________ Winery: ______

	1	2	3	4	5
Apparence					
Aroma					
Body					
Taste					
Finish					

Aging (years)

0-5 ○ 5-10 ○ 10-15 ○ +15 ○

Review

Tasting Experience ☆ ☆ ☆ ☆ ☆

Quality-Price Ratio ☆ ☆ ☆ ☆ ☆

Buy it again ? ______________

Notes

____

____

____

N° ____

Wine name: ________________________________

Red / Rosé / White (circle one) Vintage: ____________

Varietal: ____________________ Alcohol %: ____________

Region/Country: ______________ Winery: ____________

	1	2	3	4	5
Apparence					
Aroma					
Body					
Taste					
Finish					

Aging (years)

0-5 ○ 5-10 ○ 10-15 ○ +15 ○

Review

Tasting Experience ☆ ☆ ☆ ☆ ☆

Quality-Price Ratio ☆ ☆ ☆ ☆ ☆

Buy it again ? ____________________

Notes

____

____

____

N° ______

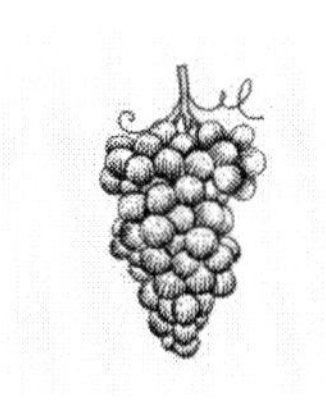

Wine name: ______

Red / Rosé / White (circle one) Vintage: ______
Varietal: ______ Alcohol %: ______
Region/Country: ______ Winery: ______

	1	2	3	4	5
Apparence					
Aroma					
Body					
Taste					
Finish					

Aging (years)

0-5 ◯ 5-10 ◯ 10-15 ◯ +15 ◯

Review

Tasting Experience ☆ ☆ ☆ ☆ ☆

Quality-Price Ratio ☆ ☆ ☆ ☆ ☆

Buy it again ? ______

Notes

______

______

______

N° ____

Wine name: ____________________

Red / Rosé / White (circle one) Vintage: ________
Varietal: ____________________ Alcohol %: ________
Region/Country: ______________ Winery: ________

	1	2	3	4	5
Apparence					
Aroma					
Body					
Taste					
Finish					

Aging (years)

0-5 ○ 5-10 ○ 10-15 ○ +15 ○

Review

Tasting Experience ☆ ☆ ☆ ☆ ☆

Quality-Price Ratio ☆ ☆ ☆ ☆ ☆

Buy it again ? ____________________

Notes

____

____

____

N° ______

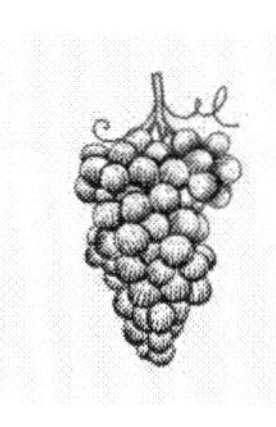

Wine name: ______________________

Red / Rosé / White (circle one) Vintage: __________
Varietal: ______________ Alcohol %: __________
Region/Country: __________ Winery: __________

	1	2	3	4	5
Apparence					
Aroma					
Body					
Taste					
Finish					

Aging (years)

0-5 ○ 5-10 ○ 10-15 ○ +15 ○

Review

Tasting Experience ☆ ☆ ☆ ☆ ☆

Quality-Price Ratio ☆ ☆ ☆ ☆ ☆

Buy it again ? ______________

Notes

____

____

____

N° ____

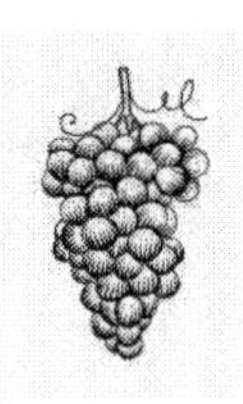

Wine name: ______________________________

Red / Rosé / White (circle one) Vintage: __________

Varietal: ____________________ Alcohol %: __________

Region/Country: ______________ Winery: __________

	1	2	3	4	5
Apparence					
Aroma					
Body					
Taste					
Finish					

Aging (years)

0-5 ○ 5-10 ○ 10-15 ○ +15 ○

Review

Tasting Experience ☆ ☆ ☆ ☆ ☆

Quality-Price Ratio ☆ ☆ ☆ ☆ ☆

Buy it again ? ____________________

Notes

____

____

____

N° ____

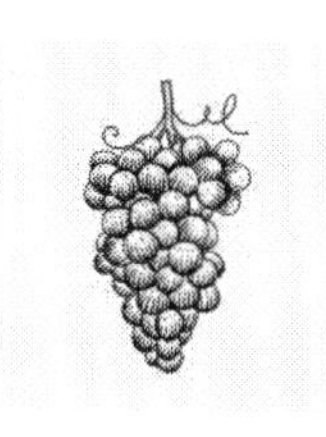

Wine name: ______________________

Red / Rosé / White (circle one) Vintage: __________

Varietal: __________________ Alcohol %: __________

Region/Country: ____________ Winery: __________

	1	2	3	4	5
Apparence					
Aroma					
Body					
Taste					
Finish					

Aging (years)

0-5 ○ 5-10 ○ 10-15 ○ +15 ○

Review

Tasting Experience ☆ ☆ ☆ ☆ ☆

Quality-Price Ratio ☆ ☆ ☆ ☆ ☆

Buy it again ? ______________________

Notes

____

____

____

N° ____

Wine name: ____________________

Red / Rosé / White (circle one) Vintage: ________
Varietal: ____________ Alcohol %: ________
Region/Country: ________ Winery: ________

	1	2	3	4	5
Apparence					
Aroma					
Body					
Taste					
Finish					

Aging (years)

0-5 ○ 5-10 ○ 10-15 ○ +15 ○

Review

Tasting Experience ☆ ☆ ☆ ☆ ☆

Quality-Price Ratio ☆ ☆ ☆ ☆ ☆

Buy it again ? ____________

Notes

____

____

____

N° ____

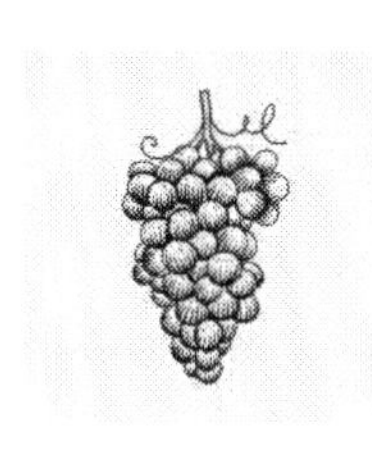

Wine name: ______________________________

Red / Rosé / White (circle one) Vintage: ____________
Varietal: ____________________ Alcohol %: ____________
Region/Country: ____________ Winery: ____________

	1	2	3	4	5
Apparence					
Aroma					
Body					
Taste					
Finish					

Aging (years)

0-5 ○ 5-10 ○ 10-15 ○ +15 ○

Review

Tasting Experience ☆ ☆ ☆ ☆ ☆

Quality-Price Ratio ☆ ☆ ☆ ☆ ☆

Buy it again ? ______________________

Notes

____

____

____

N° ____

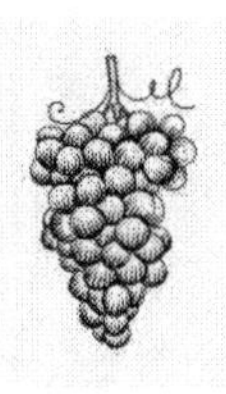

Wine name: ______________________

Red / Rosé / White (circle one) Vintage: ________
Varietal: ________________ Alcohol %: ________
Region/Country: ____________ Winery: ________

	1	2	3	4	5
Apparence					
Aroma					
Body					
Taste					
Finish					

Aging (years)

0-5 ○ 5-10 ○ 10-15 ○ +15 ○

Review

Tasting Experience ☆ ☆ ☆ ☆ ☆

Quality-Price Ratio ☆ ☆ ☆ ☆ ☆

Buy it again ? ________________

Notes

____

____

____

N° ____

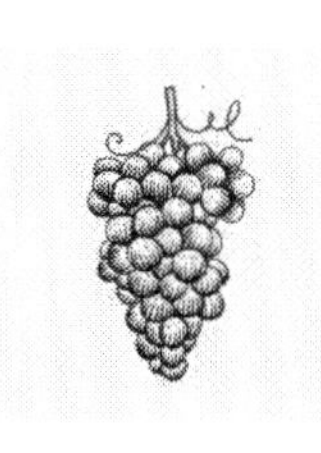

Wine name: ____________________

Red / Rosé / White (circle one) Vintage: ____________
Varietal: ____________ Alcohol %: ____________
Region/Country: ____________ Winery: ____________

	1	2	3	4	5
Apparence					
Aroma					
Body					
Taste					
Finish					

Aging (years)

0-5 ○ 5-10 ○ 10-15 ○ +15 ○

Review

Tasting Experience ☆ ☆ ☆ ☆ ☆

Quality-Price Ratio ☆ ☆ ☆ ☆ ☆

Buy it again ? ____________

Notes

____

____

____

N° ____

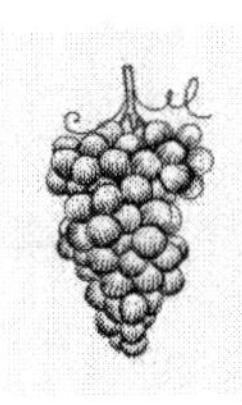

Wine name: ________________________

Red / Rosé / White (circle one) Vintage: ____________

Varietal: ____________________ Alcohol %: ____________

Region/Country: ______________ Winery: ____________

	1	2	3	4	5
Apparence					
Aroma					
Body					
Taste					
Finish					

Aging (years)

0-5 ○ 5-10 ○ 10-15 ○ +15 ○

Review

Tasting Experience ☆ ☆ ☆ ☆ ☆

Quality-Price Ratio ☆ ☆ ☆ ☆ ☆

Buy it again ? ____________________

Notes

____

____

____

N° ______

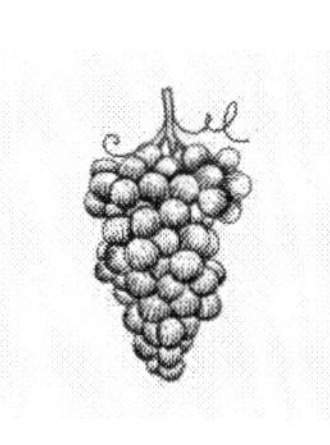

Wine name: ______________________________

Red / Rosé / White (circle one) Vintage: ______________

Varietal: ______________________ Alcohol %: ______________

Region/Country: ______________ Winery: ______________

	1	2	3	4	5
Apparence					
Aroma					
Body					
Taste					
Finish					

Aging (years)

0-5 ◯ 5-10 ◯ 10-15 ◯ +15 ◯

Review

Tasting Experience ☆ ☆ ☆ ☆ ☆

Quality-Price Ratio ☆ ☆ ☆ ☆ ☆

Buy it again ? ______________________

Notes

____

____

____

N° ______

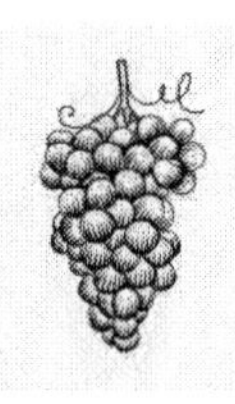

Wine name: ______

Red / Rosé / White (circle one) Vintage: ______
Varietal: ______ Alcohol %: ______
Region/Country: ______ Winery: ______

	1	2	3	4	5
Apparence					
Aroma					
Body					
Taste					
Finish					

Aging (years)

0-5 ○ 5-10 ○ 10-15 ○ +15 ○

Review

Tasting Experience ☆ ☆ ☆ ☆ ☆

Quality-Price Ratio ☆ ☆ ☆ ☆ ☆

Buy it again ? ______

Notes

______

______

______

N° ______

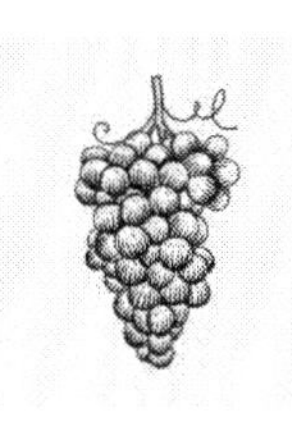

Wine name: ______________________

Red / Rosé / White (circle one) Vintage: __________

Varietal: __________________ Alcohol %: __________

Region/Country: ____________ Winery: __________

	1	2	3	4	5
Apparence					
Aroma					
Body					
Taste					
Finish					

Aging (years)

0-5 ○ 5-10 ○ 10-15 ○ +15 ○

Review

Tasting Experience ☆ ☆ ☆ ☆ ☆

Quality-Price Ratio ☆ ☆ ☆ ☆ ☆

Buy it again ? ______________

Notes

____

____

____

N° ____

Wine name: ______________________

Red / Rosé / White (circle one) Vintage: ____________

Varietal: ______________________ Alcohol %: ____________

Region/Country: ______________ Winery: ____________

	1	2	3	4	5
Apparence					
Aroma					
Body					
Taste					
Finish					

Aging (years)

0-5 ◯ 5-10 ◯ 10-15 ◯ +15 ◯

Review

Tasting Experience ☆ ☆ ☆ ☆ ☆

Quality-Price Ratio ☆ ☆ ☆ ☆ ☆

Buy it again ? ______________________

Notes

____

____

____

N° ____

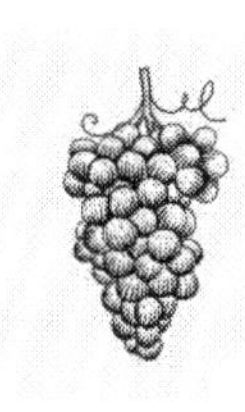

Wine name: ____________________

Red / Rosé / White (circle one) Vintage: ____________
Varietal: ____________ Alcohol %: ____________
Region/Country: ____________ Winery: ____________

	1	2	3	4	5
Apparence					
Aroma					
Body					
Taste					
Finish					

Aging (years)

0-5 ○ 5-10 ○ 10-15 ○ +15 ○

Review

Tasting Experience ☆ ☆ ☆ ☆ ☆

Quality-Price Ratio ☆ ☆ ☆ ☆ ☆

Buy it again ? ____________

Notes

____

____

____

N° ____

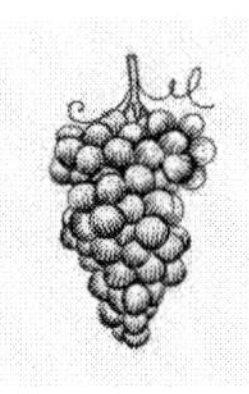

Wine name: ____________________

Red / Rosé / White (circle one) Vintage: ____________
Varietal: ____________ Alcohol %: ____________
Region/Country: ____________ Winery: ____________

	1	2	3	4	5
Apparence					
Aroma					
Body					
Taste					
Finish					

Aging (years)

0-5 ○ 5-10 ○ 10-15 ○ +15 ○

Review

Tasting Experience ☆ ☆ ☆ ☆ ☆

Quality-Price Ratio ☆ ☆ ☆ ☆ ☆

Buy it again ? ____________

Notes

____

____

____

N° ____

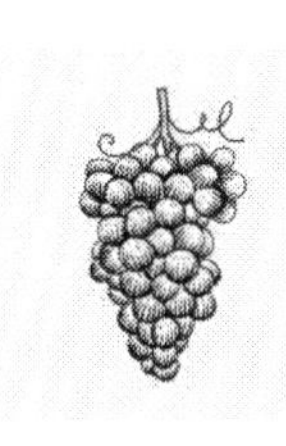

Wine name: ______________________________

Red / Rosé / White (circle one) Vintage: ____________

Varietal: ____________ Alcohol %: ____________

Region/Country: ____________ Winery: ____________

	1	2	3	4	5
Apparence					
Aroma					
Body					
Taste					
Finish					

Aging (years)

0-5 ○ 5-10 ○ 10-15 ○ +15 ○

Review

Tasting Experience ☆ ☆ ☆ ☆ ☆

Quality-Price Ratio ☆ ☆ ☆ ☆ ☆

Buy it again ? ____________

Notes

____

____

____

N° ____

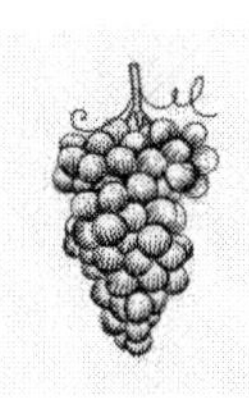

Wine name: ______________________

Red / Rosé / White (circle one) Vintage: ________
Varietal: ______________ Alcohol %: ________
Region/Country: __________ Winery: ________

	1	2	3	4	5
Apparence					
Aroma					
Body					
Taste					
Finish					

Aging (years)

0-5 ○ 5-10 ○ 10-15 ○ +15 ○

Review

Tasting Experience ☆ ☆ ☆ ☆ ☆

Quality-Price Ratio ☆ ☆ ☆ ☆ ☆

Buy it again ? ______________

Notes

____

____

____

N° ____

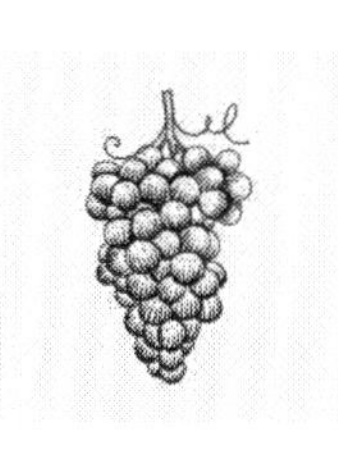

Wine name: ______________________

Red / Rosé / White (circle one) Vintage: ____________
Varietal: ____________________ Alcohol %: ____________
Region/Country: ____________ Winery: ____________

	1	2	3	4	5
Apparence					
Aroma					
Body					
Taste					
Finish					

Aging (years)

0-5 ○ 5-10 ○ 10-15 ○ +15 ○

Review

Tasting Experience ☆ ☆ ☆ ☆ ☆

Quality-Price Ratio ☆ ☆ ☆ ☆ ☆

Buy it again ? ____________________

Notes

____

____

____

N° ______

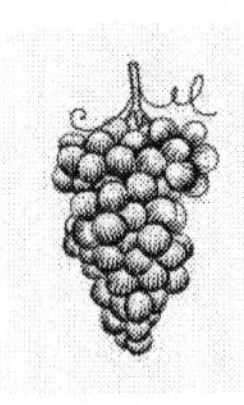

Wine name: ______________________

Red / Rosé / White (circle one) Vintage: ______
Varietal: ______________ Alcohol %: ______
Region/Country: __________ Winery: ______

	1	2	3	4	5
Apparence					
Aroma					
Body					
Taste					
Finish					

Aging (years)

0-5 ◯ 5-10 ◯ 10-15 ◯ +15 ◯

Review

Tasting Experience ☆ ☆ ☆ ☆ ☆

Quality-Price Ratio ☆ ☆ ☆ ☆ ☆

Buy it again ? ______________

Notes

____

____

____

N° _____

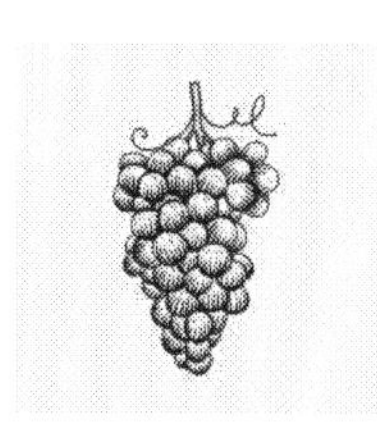

Wine name: ____________________

Red / Rosé / White (circle one) Vintage: __________

Varietal: ____________ Alcohol %: __________

Region/Country: ____________ Winery: __________

	1	2	3	4	5
Apparence					
Aroma					
Body					
Taste					
Finish					

Aging (years)

0-5 ○ 5-10 ○ 10-15 ○ +15 ○

Review

Tasting Experience ☆ ☆ ☆ ☆ ☆

Quality-Price Ratio ☆ ☆ ☆ ☆ ☆

Buy it again ? ____________

Notes

____

____

____

N° ______

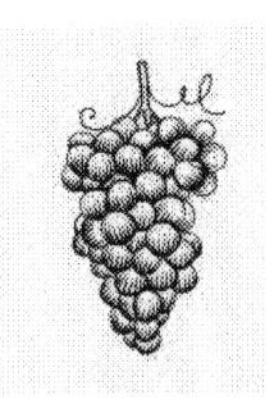

Wine name: ____________________

Red / Rosé / White (circle one) Vintage: __________
Varietal: __________________ Alcohol %: __________
Region/Country: ______________ Winery: __________

	1	2	3	4	5
Apparence					
Aroma					
Body					
Taste					
Finish					

Aging (years)

0-5 ○ 5-10 ○ 10-15 ○ +15 ○

Review

Tasting Experience ☆ ☆ ☆ ☆ ☆

Quality-Price Ratio ☆ ☆ ☆ ☆ ☆

Buy it again ? ______________

Notes

____

____

____

N° ____

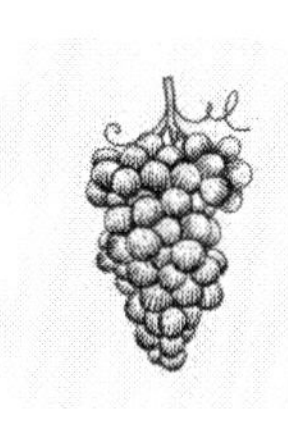

Wine name: ______________________________

Red / Rosé / White (circle one) Vintage: ____________
Varietal: ____________________ Alcohol %: ____________
Region/Country: ______________ Winery: ____________

	1	2	3	4	5
Apparence					
Aroma					
Body					
Taste					
Finish					

Aging (years)

0-5 ○ 5-10 ○ 10-15 ○ +15 ○

Review

Tasting Experience ☆ ☆ ☆ ☆ ☆

Quality-Price Ratio ☆ ☆ ☆ ☆ ☆

Buy it again ? ____________________

Notes

____

____

____

N° ____

Wine name: ______________________

Red / Rosé / White (circle one) Vintage: ____________
Varietal: ____________ Alcohol %: ____________
Region/Country: ____________ Winery: ____________

	1	2	3	4	5
Apparence					
Aroma					
Body					
Taste					
Finish					

Aging (years)

0-5 ● 5-10 ● 10-15 ● +15 ●

Review

Tasting Experience ☆ ☆ ☆ ☆ ☆

Quality-Price Ratio ☆ ☆ ☆ ☆ ☆

Buy it again ? ____________

Notes

____

____

____

N° ____

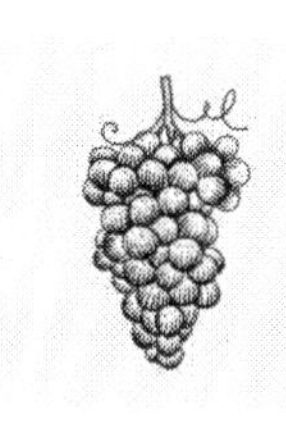

Wine name: ______________________

Red / Rosé / White (circle one) Vintage: __________
Varietal: ______________ Alcohol %: __________
Region/Country: __________ Winery: __________

	1	2	3	4	5
Apparence					
Aroma					
Body					
Taste					
Finish					

Aging (years)

0-5 ◯ 5-10 ◯ 10-15 ◯ +15 ◯

Review

Tasting Experience ☆ ☆ ☆ ☆ ☆

Quality-Price Ratio ☆ ☆ ☆ ☆ ☆

Buy it again ? ______________

Notes

____

____

____

N° ____

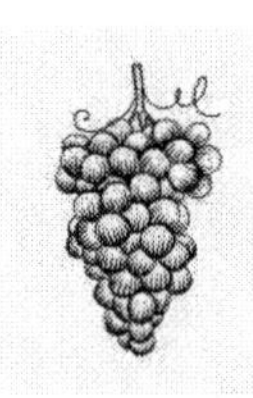

Wine name: ______________________

Red / Rosé / White (circle one) Vintage: ________

Varietal: ________________ Alcohol %: ________

Region/Country: ________ Winery: ________

	1	2	3	4	5
Apparence					
Aroma					
Body					
Taste					
Finish					

Aging (years)

0-5 ◯ 5-10 ◯ 10-15 ◯ +15 ◯

Review

Tasting Experience ☆ ☆ ☆ ☆ ☆

Quality-Price Ratio ☆ ☆ ☆ ☆ ☆

Buy it again ? ________________

Notes

____

____

____

N° ______

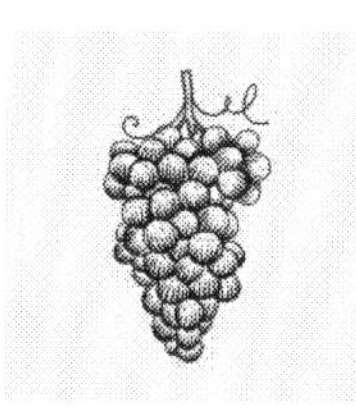

Vine name: ______

?ed / Rosé / White (circle one) Vintage: ______

/arietal: ______ Alcohol %: ______

?egion/Country: ______ Winery: ______

	1	2	3	4	5
Apparence					
Aroma					
3ody					
'aste					
Finish					

Aging (years)

0-5 ○ 5-10 ○ 10-15 ○ +15 ○

?eview

'asting Experience ☆ ☆ ☆ ☆ ☆

Quality-Price Ratio ☆ ☆ ☆ ☆ ☆

3uy it again ? ______

Notes

______

______

______

N° ______

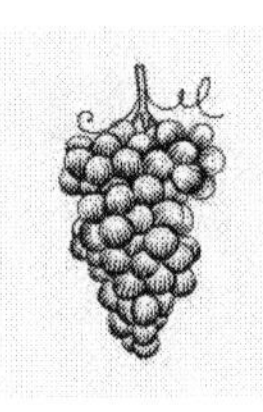

Wine name: ______________________

Red / Rosé / White (circle one) Vintage: ______
Varietal: ______________ Alcohol %: ______
Region/Country: __________ Winery: ______

	1	2	3	4	5
Apparence					
Aroma					
Body					
Taste					
Finish					

Aging (years)

0-5 ○ 5-10 ○ 10-15 ○ +15 ○

Review

Tasting Experience ☆ ☆ ☆ ☆ ☆

Quality-Price Ratio ☆ ☆ ☆ ☆ ☆

Buy it again ? ______________

Notes

____

____

____

N° ____

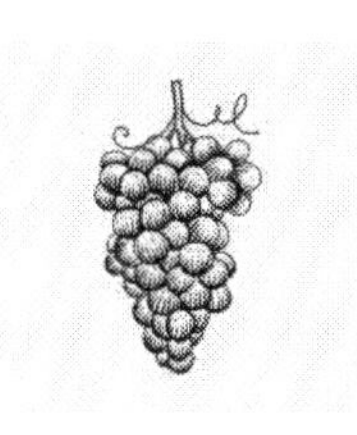

Wine name: ____________________

Red / Rosé / White (circle one) Vintage: ____________
Varietal: ____________________ Alcohol %: ____________
Region/Country: ____________ Winery: ____________

	1	2	3	4	5
Apparence					
Aroma					
Body					
Taste					
Finish					

Aging (years)

0-5 ○ 5-10 ○ 10-15 ○ +15 ○

Review

Tasting Experience ☆ ☆ ☆ ☆ ☆

Quality-Price Ratio ☆ ☆ ☆ ☆ ☆

Buy it again ? ____________________

Notes

____

____

____

N° ____

Wine name: ____________________

Red / Rosé / White (circle one) Vintage: ____________
Varietal: ____________ Alcohol %: ____________
Region/Country: ____________ Winery: ____________

	1	2	3	4	5
Apparence					
Aroma					
Body					
Taste					
Finish					

Aging (years)

0-5 ○ 5-10 ○ 10-15 ○ +15 ○

Review

Tasting Experience ☆ ☆ ☆ ☆ ☆

Quality-Price Ratio ☆ ☆ ☆ ☆ ☆

Buy it again ? ____________

Notes

____

____

____

N° ____

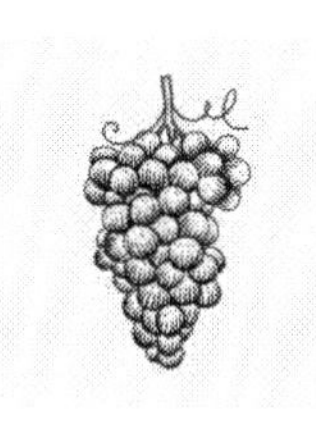

Wine name: ____________________

Red / Rosé / White (circle one) Vintage: ____________
Varietal: ____________ Alcohol %: ____________
Region/Country: ____________ Winery: ____________

	1	2	3	4	5
Apparence					
Aroma					
Body					
Taste					
Finish					

Aging (years)

0-5 ○ 5-10 ○ 10-15 ○ +15 ○

Review

Tasting Experience ☆ ☆ ☆ ☆ ☆

Quality-Price Ratio ☆ ☆ ☆ ☆ ☆

Buy it again ? ____________

Notes

____

____

____

N° ______

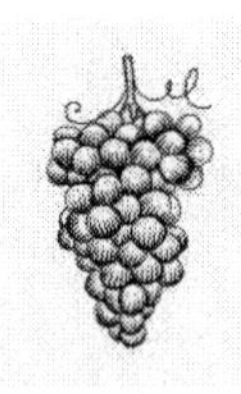

Wine name: ______________________________

Red / Rosé / White (circle one) Vintage: ____________
Varietal: ____________________ Alcohol %: ____________
Region/Country: ____________ Winery: ____________

	1	2	3	4	5
Apparence					
Aroma					
Body					
Taste					
Finish					

Aging (years)

0-5 ○ 5-10 ○ 10-15 ○ +15 ○

Review

Tasting Experience ☆ ☆ ☆ ☆ ☆

Quality-Price Ratio ☆ ☆ ☆ ☆ ☆

Buy it again ? ____________________

Notes

____

____

____

N° ____

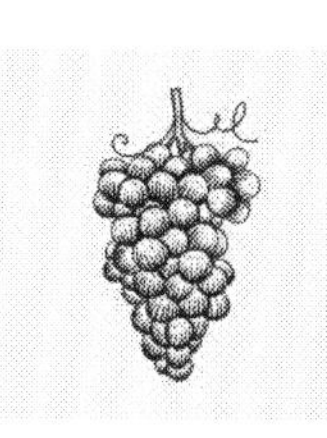

Wine name: ______________________________

Red / Rosé / White (circle one) Vintage: ____________
Varietal: ____________________ Alcohol %: ____________
Region/Country: ____________ Winery: ____________

	1	2	3	4	5
Apparence					
Aroma					
Body					
Taste					
Finish					

Aging (years)

0-5 ○ 5-10 ○ 10-15 ○ +15 ○

Review

Tasting Experience ☆ ☆ ☆ ☆ ☆

Quality-Price Ratio ☆ ☆ ☆ ☆ ☆

Buy it again ? ____________________

Notes

____

____

____

No _____

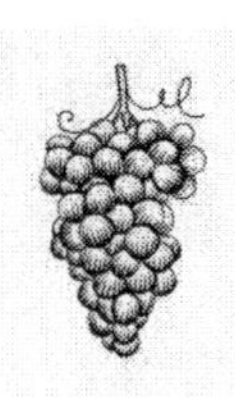

Wine name: ______________________

Red / Rosé / White (circle one) Vintage: __________
Varietal: ______________ Alcohol %: __________
Region/Country: ______________ Winery: __________

	1	2	3	4	5
Apparence					
Aroma					
Body					
Taste					
Finish					

Aging (years)

0-5 ○ 5-10 ○ 10-15 ○ +15 ○

Review

Tasting Experience ☆ ☆ ☆ ☆ ☆

Quality-Price Ratio ☆ ☆ ☆ ☆ ☆

Buy it again ? ______________

Notes

____

____

____

N° ____

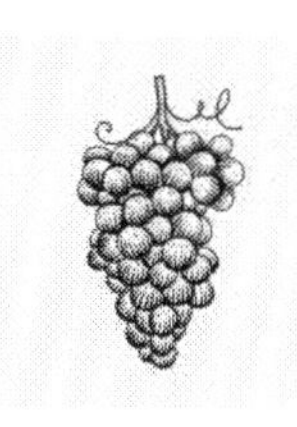

Wine name: ____________________

Red / Rosé / White (circle one) Vintage: ____________
Varietal: ____________ Alcohol %: ____________
Region/Country: ____________ Winery: ____________

	1	2	3	4	5
Apparence					
Aroma					
Body					
Taste					
Finish					

Aging (years)

0-5 ○ 5-10 ○ 10-15 ○ +15 ○

Review

Tasting Experience ☆ ☆ ☆ ☆ ☆

Quality-Price Ratio ☆ ☆ ☆ ☆ ☆

Buy it again ? ____________

Notes

____

____

____

N° ____

Wine name: ______________________

Red / Rosé / White (circle one) Vintage: __________
Varietal: ______________________ Alcohol %: __________
Region/Country: ______________ Winery: __________

	1	2	3	4	5
Apparence					
Aroma					
Body					
Taste					
Finish					

Aging (years)

0-5 ◯ 5-10 ◯ 10-15 ◯ +15 ◯

Review

Tasting Experience ☆ ☆ ☆ ☆ ☆
Quality-Price Ratio ☆ ☆ ☆ ☆ ☆
Buy it again ? ______________________

Notes

____

____

____

N° ______

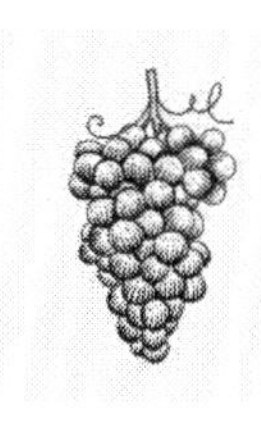

Wine name: ______________________________

Red / Rosé / White (circle one) Vintage: ____________
Varietal: ____________________ Alcohol %: ____________
Region/Country: ____________ Winery: ____________

	1	2	3	4	5
Apparence					
Aroma					
Body					
Taste					
Finish					

Aging (years)

0-5 ○ 5-10 ○ 10-15 ○ +15 ○

Review

Tasting Experience ☆ ☆ ☆ ☆ ☆

Quality-Price Ratio ☆ ☆ ☆ ☆ ☆

Buy it again ? ____________________

Notes

____

____

____

N° ____

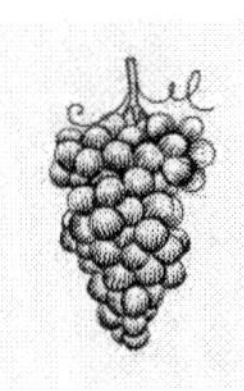

Wine name: ____________________

Red / Rosé / White (circle one) Vintage: ____________
Varietal: ____________________ Alcohol %: ____________
Region/Country: ______________ Winery: ____________

	1	2	3	4	5
Apparence					
Aroma					
Body					
Taste					
Finish					

Aging (years)

0-5 ○ 5-10 ○ 10-15 ○ +15 ○

Review

Tasting Experience ☆ ☆ ☆ ☆ ☆

Quality-Price Ratio ☆ ☆ ☆ ☆ ☆

Buy it again ? ____________________

Notes

____

____

____

N° ____

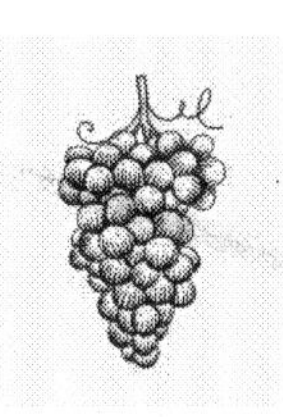

Wine name: ____________________

Red / Rosé / White (circle one) Vintage: ____________

Varietal: ____________ Alcohol %: ____________

Region/Country: ____________ Winery: ____________

	1	2	3	4	5
Apparence					
Aroma					
Body					
Taste					
Finish					

Aging (years)

0-5 ○ 5-10 ○ 10-15 ○ +15 ○

Review

Tasting Experience ☆ ☆ ☆ ☆ ☆

Quality-Price Ratio ☆ ☆ ☆ ☆ ☆

Buy it again ? ____________

Notes

____

____

____

N° ____

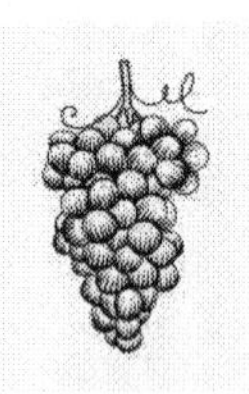

Wine name: ____________________

Red / Rosé / White (circle one) Vintage: ____________
Varietal: ____________ Alcohol %: ____________
Region/Country: ____________ Winery: ____________

	1	2	3	4	5
Apparence					
Aroma					
Body					
Taste					
Finish					

Aging (years)

0-5 ○ 5-10 ○ 10-15 ○ +15 ○

Review

Tasting Experience ☆ ☆ ☆ ☆ ☆

Quality-Price Ratio ☆ ☆ ☆ ☆ ☆

Buy it again ? ____________

Notes

____

____

____

N° ______

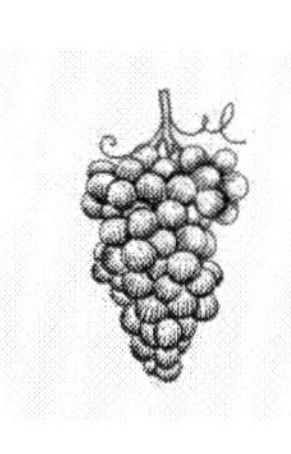

Wine name: ______________________________

Red / Rosé / White (circle one) Vintage: ____________
Varietal: ____________________ Alcohol %: ____________
Region/Country: ____________ Winery: ____________

	1	2	3	4	5
Apparence					
Aroma					
Body					
Taste					
Finish					

Aging (years)

0-5 ◯ 5-10 ◯ 10-15 ◯ +15 ◯

Review

Tasting Experience ☆ ☆ ☆ ☆ ☆
Quality-Price Ratio ☆ ☆ ☆ ☆ ☆
Buy it again ? ____________________

Notes

____

____

____

N° ______

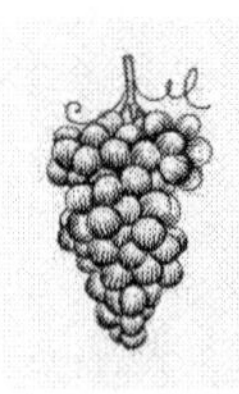

Wine name: ______________________

Red / Rosé / White (circle one) Vintage: __________
Varietal: ______________ Alcohol %: __________
Region/Country: ______________ Winery: __________

	1	2	3	4	5
Apparence					
Aroma					
Body					
Taste					
Finish					

Aging (years)

0-5 ○ 5-10 ○ 10-15 ○ +15 ○

Review

Tasting Experience ☆ ☆ ☆ ☆ ☆

Quality-Price Ratio ☆ ☆ ☆ ☆ ☆

Buy it again ? ______________

Notes

____

____

____

N° ____

Wine name: ______________________

Red / Rosé / White (circle one) Vintage: ____________

Varietal: ____________ Alcohol %: ____________

Region/Country: ____________ Winery: ____________

	1	2	3	4	5
Apparence					
Aroma					
Body					
Taste					
Finish					

Aging (years)

0-5 ○ 5-10 ○ 10-15 ○ +15 ○

Review

Tasting Experience ☆ ☆ ☆ ☆ ☆

Quality-Price Ratio ☆ ☆ ☆ ☆ ☆

Buy it again ? ____________

Notes

____

____

____

Made in the USA
Columbia, SC
25 October 2023